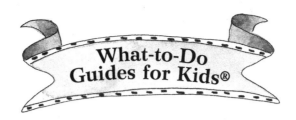

What-to-Do Guides for Kids®

What to Do When You

GRUMBLE

TOO MUCH

A Kid's
Guide to
Overcoming
Negativity

by Dawn Huebner, Ph.D.

illustrated by Bonnie Matthews

MAGINATION PRESS • WASHINGTON, D.C.

Published by
M A G I N A T I O N   P R E S S
An Educational Publishing Foundation Book
American Psychological Association
750 First Street, NE
Washington, DC 20002

For more information about our books, including a complete catalog, please write to us,
call 1-800-374-2721, or visit our website at www.maginationpress.com.

Library of Congress Cataloging-in-Publication Data

Huebner, Dawn.
What to do when you grumble too much : a kid's guide to overcoming negativity /
by Dawn Huebner ; illustrated by Bonnie Matthews.
p. cm. – (What-to-do guides for kids)
Summary: "Teaches school-age children cognitive-behavioral techniques to reduce and overcome
negativity, through writing and drawing activities and self-help exercises and strategies.
Includes introduction for parents"–Provided by publisher.
ISBN-13: 978-1-59147-450-0 (pbk. : alk. paper)
ISBN-10: 1-59147-450-7 (pbk. : alk. paper)
1. Negativism–Juvenile literature. I. Matthews, Bonnie. II. Title. III. Series.
BF698.35.N44H84 2006
155.2'32–dc22   2006008209

Manufactured in the United States of America
10 9 8 7 6

CONTENTS

Introduction to Parents and Caregivers

Some children seem to have radar tuned in to what is *wrong* in any given situation. No matter how much is right, they have a way of noticing and commenting on every little problem, no matter how small or inconsequential.

Parenting a child who zooms in on problems, a child who often has a negative view, is hard work. If you are the parent of a child who "grumbles too much," you are probably nodding your head in agreement. You want your child to be happy, and you have probably worn yourself out trying to make that happen. You have bought the latest toys, waited in amusement park lines, laughed at marginally funny jokes. You have hosted play dates, lost at Go Fish, cooked endless bowls of macaroni and cheese, and repeatedly gone above and beyond the call of duty for the sake of your child. And your child probably has been happy.

Children who tend toward the negative are actually often happy, as long as everything is going well. And therein lies the catch, because in real life, there are glitches. One of the rides at the amusement park is out of commission, you forget to pick up the blueberry yogurt, a school friend chooses to sit with someone else. And that's when the grumbling (and worse) begins. In the life of a child whose thinking quickly turns negative, a small mishap can shatter an afternoon.

Children who tend toward negativity are masters at noticing problems. It's as if deviations, imperfections, and injustices jump out at them, magnified a hundredfold. They feel compelled to point out what is wrong or unfair. These children are experts at making mountains out of molehills, and typically grow increasingly angry when attempts are made to talk them out of their point of view.

Negativity is not the same as sadness, nor should the term be used to describe children struggling to make sense of painful life events such as a house fire, the death of a pet, or a divorce. Negativity is also different from depression, which is characterized by ongoing sadness and irritability. Negativity is, instead, a cognitive style. It is a way of thinking—not just a mood, but an approach to life.

Negativity is characterized by the repeated tendency to focus on what is wrong, even when there is plenty that is right. Children with a negative tendency will overlook a table full of gifts to wonder why they didn't get a particular toy. They will pout when, after a full day of child-centered activities, you say no to a movie rental. They are often happy, but their contentment is fragile. Even in the absence of significant stressors, they grumble a lot.

It's hard to sympathize with grumbling, and most parents don't. On the best of days, grumbling brings a bewildered parental response along the lines of "Why are you so upset?" or an attempt at logic, such as, "But you like peanut butter, too. Why don't you have that, instead?" On the worst of days, negativity provokes anger: "You are just impossible. Nothing is ever good enough for you, is it? I don't know why I bother." And on good days and bad days, in calm tones and exasperated tones, parents hit their heads against the brick wall of negativity.

Now the goal, as you know, is not simply

4

to end the grumbling. Children whose thinking quickly turns negative are good at fuming in silence, too. The goal is to teach these children about negativity and to motivate them to do something about it. The goal is also to help them become more resilient in the face of disappointment and to provide them with the skills they need to focus on the positive rather than staying mired in the negative.

Children mired in negativity don't choose to have that cognitive style; most have no idea what negativity even means. And they are notoriously defensive about their negativity. "I do not grumble too much!" might be your child's first reaction to seeing this book. But as you begin reading together, your child will get hooked. *What to Do When You Grumble Too Much* carefully, sympathetically, and humorously guides children through an understanding of negativity and its pitfalls. It recognizes that children with lots of negative thoughts often feel stuck and unhappy. And, importantly, it tells them what to do, using exercises and explanations they will understand.

The strategies presented in this book are based on cognitive-behavioral principles used extensively by therapists. All have been adapted for use by children 6 to 12 years old. *What to Do When You Grumble Too Much* will be most effective when read by a parent and child together. Take your time. Sit in a comfortable spot, with writing and drawing supplies readily available. Read a chapter or two at a time, looking at the pictures and doing the activities as directed. Talk with your child about the examples, and bring them up between reading sessions. Children need time to absorb new ideas and to practice new strategies. Change happens a little bit at a time.

By presenting this book, you are asking your child to experiment with new ways of thinking. You will need to change, too. No longer try to talk your child out of negativity. Don't give logical explanations. And try not to get angry. Instead, begin to identify negativity for what it is.

Rather than responding to the specifics of your child's complaints, sympathize with how he or she is feeling. Say, "You sound really upset" or "Wow, I can tell that is really bothering you." Then use the examples in this book to remind your child to use the new techniques. Encourage all steps in the right direction. Use humor in a way that is silly, not insulting. Project an air of confidence in your child's ability to learn and to choose this new way of thinking. By envisioning your child's success, you help to make that success a reality.

It is not unusual for negativity to run in families. If you tend to be a negative thinker yourself, you might try to approach these exercises together with your child. If you find, however, that your feelings and reactions are too hard to change, you may want to seek professional guidance in working with your child. And if negativity is significantly interfering with your child's life, please talk to your child's pediatrician or to a mental health specialist right away. For some children, it will be best to use this book as a companion to therapy.

The good news for both adults and children is that negativity is a style that can be modified through the cognitive-behavioral strategies described in this book. Your child can learn to recognize and shift out of a negative mode. It takes some practice, but once your child gets the hang of it, things get a whole lot easier. And as you know, positive thinking is very reinforcing. It feels better, it works better, and best of all, it makes kids (and their parents!) much, much happier.

CHAPTER ONE

Are You Getting Stuck?

Have you ever run an obstacle course?

An obstacle course, as you know, is a route full of tricky spots. There are hurdles to jump over, tubes to wiggle through, boards to balance on, and cones to race around.

Most kids look at an obstacle course and think, "Wow! That looks like fun." They set off at full speed, leaping over hurdles and dodging cones.

In an obstacle course, each obstacle is a mini-adventure waiting to be conquered.

Draw yourself getting ready to run this obstacle course. Then draw a line that shows how you would get over or through the obstacles.

Now imagine a child who loves to run but has never seen an obstacle course. This child sets off at top speed and reaches the first hurdle.

Wait a minute!
The hurdle is in his way.

The child stops and stares at it.
The hurdle doesn't move.
So the child does what many
children do when something
is in their way. He gets **MAD**.

The hurdle doesn't move.

"It's not fair!" he says.

The hurdle still doesn't move. Now he's really mad, so he kicks the hurdle. The hurdle still doesn't move. (Of course not, it's a hurdle.)

"That stupid hurdle!" he thinks. "It's blocking my way and now it hurt my toe."

The child stands there for a long time, yelling at and complaining about the hurdle.

What advice can you give the child who is stuck behind the hurdle? (Hint: what would you do if you were running the obstacle course?)

Write your advice here.

If you wrote **JUMP THE HURDLE**, give yourself a star. You knew exactly what to do.

Did you know that life is like an obstacle course? There are lots of tricky spots to get through.

Some kids, maybe even kids like you, are especially good at spotting hurdles. But then they get stuck.

They forget that hurdles should be jumped over, and they wind up complaining about them instead. They say things like, "That's not fair!" And they feel angry or sad because there are hurdles in their way.

If you are a kid with plenty of hurdles in your path, and especially if you are a kid who has been complaining about those hurdles, this book is for you. It will teach you to see the hurdles in a new way, and to figure out how to get past them.

What Is Negativity?

Things don't always go as planned.

Your mom might say you can get the next book in your favorite mystery series, but when you get to the store, it isn't on the shelf.

Your sister is willing to play with you, but she insists on playing school and you want to play pet store.

Your grandpa takes you out to eat, but he forgets to tell the waitress to hold the tomato and now there is a big one right there on your hamburger!

Each of these situations has good parts and bad parts. Make a list of each.

Your mom says you can get the next book in your favorite mystery series, but when you get to the store, it isn't on the shelf.

Good Parts

BAD PARTS

Your sister will play with you, but she insists on playing school and you want to play pet store.

Good Parts

BAD PARTS

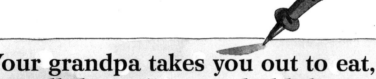

Your grandpa takes you out to eat, but he forgets to tell the waitress to hold the tomato and now there is a big one right there on your hamburger!

 Good Parts

 BAD PARTS

When there are both good parts and bad parts to a situation, you have a choice. You can focus on what is wrong and get upset about it. Or you can pay attention to the good parts.

NEGATIVITY means focusing on the bad parts.

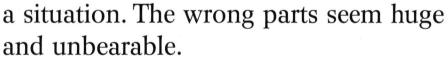

Kids with a negative focus quickly notice what is wrong in a situation. The wrong parts seem huge and unbearable.

So these kids do the only thing that makes sense to them. They complain. They say things like, "But I hate tomatoes" or "We never get to play what I want."

People who focus on the negative parts are called **PESSIMISTS**. A pessimist is someone who expects things to not work out. Pessimists are usually pretty set in their ways. When something goes wrong, they are quick to point it out. Sometimes they are so bothered by the bad parts of a situation that they can't enjoy the good parts.

How do you think negative thinkers often feel?

Who do you know who tends to be negative? Draw a picture of that person.

Some people focus mainly on the good parts of a situation. They expect good things to happen, and while they might notice what is wrong, they don't pay much attention to it. These people are called **OPTIMISTS**, or positive thinkers.

How do you think positive thinkers usually feel?

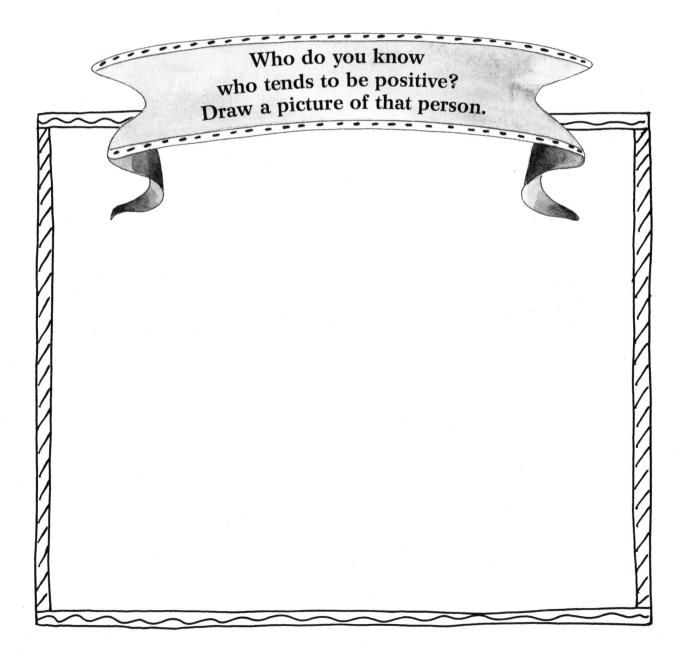

Who do you know who tends to be positive? Draw a picture of that person.

Of course, no one is always positive or always negative, but people do have a tendency to be more one way or the other.

People who tend to be negative often don't realize it. It's like they are holding a weird magnifying glass that makes bad stuff look huge and good stuff look tiny. But they don't realize that they are holding the magnifying glass. It just seems like the bad stuff really is so much bigger.

How often do you hold one of those magnifying glasses? How often is it hard to see the good in a situation because the problems seem so big? Circle your answer.

If you are negative some of the time, this book will help you learn new ways of coping when things go wrong.

If you are negative much of the time, then practicing the things you learn in this book will help you to be a happier kid.

How Does Negativity Get Started?

You might think that people who focus on negative stuff get that way because bad things always happen to them, but that isn't true.

Being positive or being negative has very little to do with what actually happens to you. Instead, it depends on how you *think* about what happens to you.

Whether you are mostly positive or mostly negative depends on the thoughts inside your head, not on what is actually going on.

How can that be?

Take a marker and fill this glass half way up with a color that shows your favorite drink. Pretend you are really thirsty.

Would you say that the glass is half full, or would you say it is half empty?

Would you notice that it is your favorite drink sitting right there, waiting for you to drink it? Or would you notice that there isn't very much in the glass?

Pretend you are a person who looks at the glass and thinks, "Yum, my favorite!" Draw a face that shows how you would feel.

Now pretend you are a person who looks at the glass and thinks, "I'm so thirsty, that's never going to be enough!" Draw a face that shows how you would feel.

It isn't the drink that makes you feel happy or grouchy. It's the thoughts inside your head that determine how you feel. Either way, there is half a glass to drink. Whether that seems like a good thing or a bad thing depends on what you are thinking.

So, is being **NEGATIVE** something a person learns, or are some people just born that way?

Scientists aren't sure, but it does seem that some people's brains are set up in a way that makes it easier for them to be happy while other people's brains zoom in on **PROBLEMS**.

To understand how this works, think for a minute about your body. Are you right-handed or left-handed? Circle the hand that you use to write with.

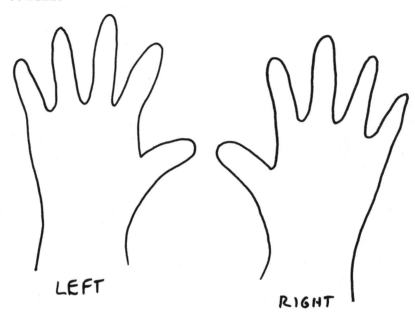

If you are right-handed, chances are the right side of your body is stronger than the left. If you need to carry something heavy, your right arm is the one to do the job.

If you are on a scooter, using one leg at a time to make yourself go, your left leg probably gets tired faster than your right. The right side is stronger on right-handed people.

It's the opposite for left-handed people. If you are left-handed, your left side is probably stronger.

Think about playing kickball. When it's your turn to kick, which leg do you use? If you are right-handed, you probably kick with your right leg. If you are left-handed, you probably kick with your left leg.

If you had to kick with your opposite leg, it would probably feel funny, and chances are good that the ball wouldn't go nearly as straight or as far as you can usually get it to go.

Why is that?

It wouldn't work out so well because you aren't used to kicking with that leg, and the muscles in that leg are probably a little weaker.

But what if you wanted to become a champion kickball player who could do expert kicks with either leg? What would you need to do?

If you wanted to train your opposite leg to kick the ball super-hard and super-far, you would need to strengthen that leg by exercising it. You would need to practice kicking with that leg lots and lots of times.

Actually, exercise can make any part of your body stronger. Think of an exercise that would make each of these parts of your body stronger. Describe it.

So, you know that exercise can strengthen your body. Did you know that the same thing is true for your brain?

If you have a brain that is stronger on the negative side, you can do brain exercises to strengthen the positive part of your brain.

Scientists have discovered that people can actually change the way their brain works by practicing certain kinds of thinking.

Practicing positive thinking strengthens the part of your brain that notices positive things. Keeping that part of your brain strong can help you feel happier.

CHAPTER FOUR

Strength and Flexibility

Some things are flexible. That means that they bend.

Draw or name three things that are flexible.

Some things are inflexible. That means they cannot bend. If you try to bend them, they will break.

Draw or name three things that are inflexible.

People are full of flexible parts. Find six parts of your body that can stretch and bend. Put a dot on the flexible parts.

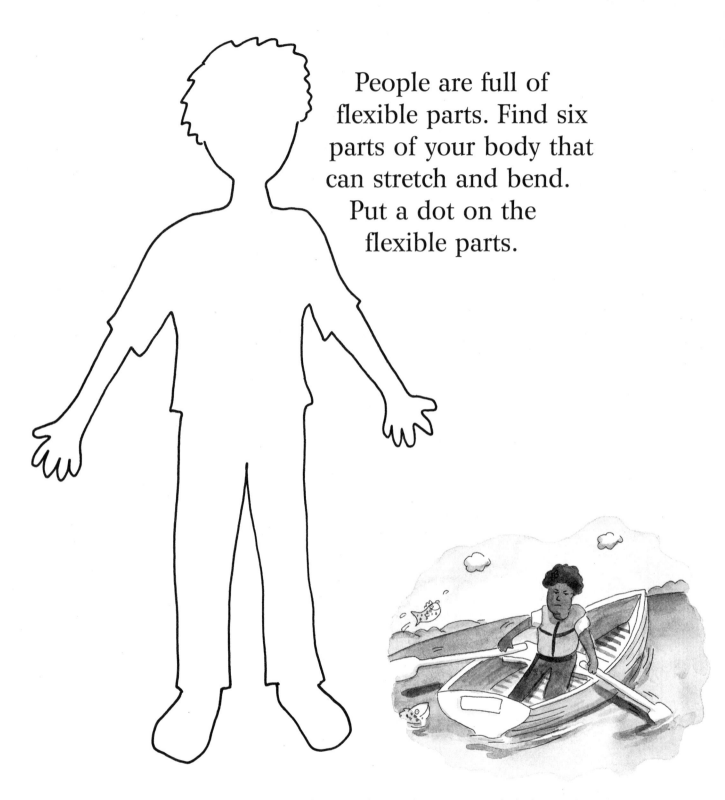

Can you imagine how hard it would be if you couldn't bend or stretch your body at all? What are some things you like to do that you couldn't do if your body wasn't flexible?

You have probably noticed that some people's bodies are more flexible than others. Let's see how flexible your body is.

First, stand up.

Now bend at your waist while you keep your legs straight, and try to touch your toes.

How far down can you get? How far down can the grown-up who is reading this with you get?

Circle where you are on this flexibility scale. Circle where the grown-up is.

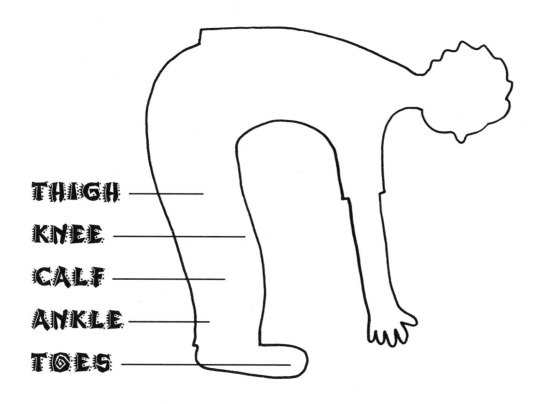

THIGH ——————

KNEE ——————

CALF ——————

ANKLE ——————

TOES ——————

What would you need to do if you wanted to be able to get all the way down to the ground?

People can make their bodies more flexible by gradually stretching. If you wanted to be able to touch your toes, you would need to practice a few times a week, each time stretching your body just a *t-i-n-y* bit past where it can already comfortably go.

If you do it too forcefully or too fast, you'll hurt yourself by straining the muscles you're trying to stretch. You need to do it just a bit at a time.

Did you know that your mind is something that can be flexible or inflexible, too? Being flexible in your mind means that you can bend or shift your thinking when you need to.

Take a look at these two children.

One has a flexible mind. That means that when something doesn't work out the way she expects it to, she doesn't get too upset. Instead, she bends her mind, makes another choice, and feels OK.

The other child has an inflexible mind. She likes things to be a certain way, and when they can't be that way, she gets upset.

Both of these children love the color blue. When it's time for lunch, their mom tells them that the blue cups are dirty. What do you think the flexible child will say? What will the inflexible child say? Which child is likely to feel happier? Circle her.

Just like having an inflexible body causes lots of problems, so does having an inflexible brain. Kids who are inflexible end up feeling frustrated and angry. When someone tries to force them to bend, they feel like they are going to break in two. Of course, inflexible kids don't really break, but they do SNAP by yelling or crying or feeling really bad inside.

Being inflexible and being negative often go together. When your brain isn't flexible, it's hard to shift away from paying attention to the bad parts. It's like the weird magnifying glass got super-glued onto your hand, making it impossible to put down.

But just like you can make your body more flexible, you can teach your brain to be more flexible too, by stretching it in new ways a little bit at a time.

You are about to learn some exercises that will stretch and strengthen your brain. Each time you practice them, your brain will become more flexible, and the parts of your brain that think in positive ways will get stronger. Having a flexible, positive brain will help you to feel happier.

Exercise #1
Jumping Hurdles

The first exercise involves something you already know about: jumping hurdles.

You have probably jumped over lots of things with your legs. How do you think you might jump something with your brain? It's actually easier than it sounds, because whether you are using your legs or your brain, you follow the same four steps.

1: See the hurdle.

2: Decide to jump it.

3: Figure out how to do it.

4: Jump!

The first two steps may seem obvious, but they are actually the most important steps of all. Imagine you were running an obstacle course and you got to the first hurdle but didn't notice it. You would crash right into it and probably wind up getting hurt.

When you have a problem, you need to see the problem correctly. Then you can decide what to do about it.

Remember the boy in the first chapter who didn't know any of this? He saw the hurdle blocking his path, and then he got stuck behind it. Actually, he got stuck because his thoughts were negative and inflexible.

He was mad about the hurdle. He thought it was unfair. It didn't even occur to him to jump the hurdle. (It's a good thing you were there to tell him.)

When you have a problem, think about that boy and how he got stuck. Think about how he stood there, complaining. It didn't do him any good.

When you're stuck behind a problem, the first thing you need to do is **SEE THE HURDLE**. You need to realize that there is a problem you're reacting to.

The next thing you need to do is **DECIDE TO JUMP**. Once you decide to jump, things get a whole lot easier.

But what does it mean to jump a problem? Jumping a problem means getting past it. It means solving the problem or shifting your attention to something else so you can move on.

YEAH!

I AM MAD AT TOM TODAY ...

WHY DID BETH DO THAT TO ME?

MOM MADE ME CLEAN MY ROOM

MY BROTHER IS ANNOYING ME TODAY

Let's review what you probably already know about solving problems.

You know that it's a good idea to begin by brainstorming. Brainstorming means coming up with lots of ideas. Brainstorming and jumping hurdles stretch your brain, keeping it nice and flexible.

See if you can brainstorm about this problem:

You want to have a friend over, but your mom has to take your sister to gymnastics.

Instead of getting mad, you think, "I'm going to jump that hurdle."

Write your ideas about how to solve the problem here.

You probably came up with lots of ways to jump the hurdle, because all kinds of solutions are possible. Here are a few more:

◉ Go to your friend's house instead.

◉ Bring your friend to gymnastics and play there.

◉ Grab a good book to read during your sister's class, and have your friend over tomorrow.

Now let's practice with some examples from your life.

Write a problem that you've had on each of the hurdles pictured below. For each problem, think of at least one way to get past it. Keep your answers realistic. Try to think of solutions that are within your power, rather than things you wish could happen or things you want other people to do.

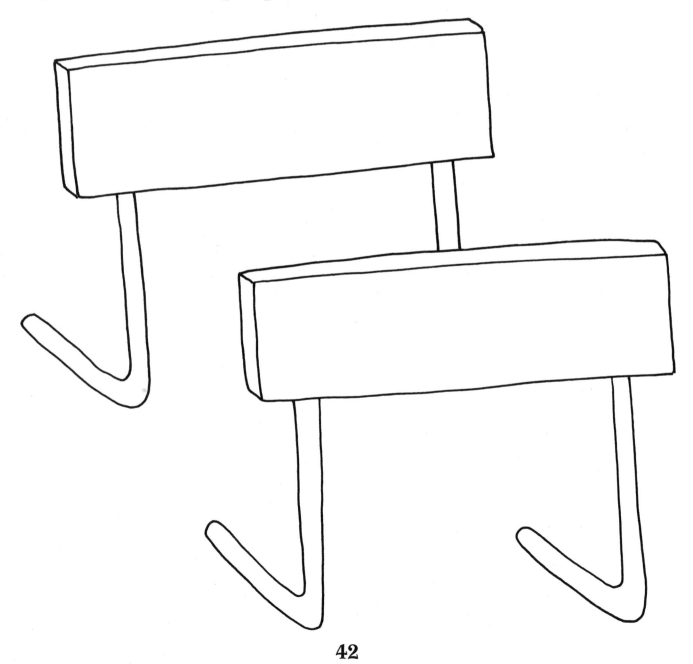

From now on when you have a problem, think about jumping hurdles. Instead of pouting or complaining or getting stuck in other ways, tell yourself, "That's a hurdle and I'm going to jump it."

Make a sign that will remind you to

JUMP!

CHAPTER SIX

Finding a Coach

Professional runners and hurdle jumpers often have a coach. A coach is someone who helps you learn how to do new things. A coach can also help you remember what to do. Someday soon you will become your own coach, but as you're learning these exercises, you might need someone to help you.

See if you can think of two or three grown-ups who might be able to coach you as you learn these brain exercises.

Write the names of your coaches here:

1. _____

2. _____

3. _____

This chapter will help you and your coaches figure out how to work together, so be sure to read it with them.

Remember that weird magnifying glass, the one that makes bad things look huge?

By the time you get to the end of this book, the magnifying glass will be gathering dust on your shelf. (In other words, you won't be holding it very much anymore.)

For now, though, you are probably still holding it a lot, because that's what you're used to doing. And whenever you hold it, the magnifying glass points directly at **THE PROBLEM**, making it seem huge.

Read each of these examples, and circle the part of the picture that shows **THE PROBLEM**. (This is where the magnifying glass would be pointing.)

You are at the roller rink for your birthday party. You and your friends skate for an hour. When it's time to eat, the waitress brings out your cake, glowing with candles, but the frosting is white, and you like chocolate best.

Yesterday you and your best friend played tag at recess. Today you're looking forward to playing again. You finish your lunch and race outside, but when you get to the playground, you see your friend jumping rope with some other kids.

You are in the car. Your brother is breathing too loud. It's driving you crazy.

Let's take another look at that last scene. So far, the magnifying glass is pointing at your brother, right? His breathing sounds worse and worse. You can hardly stand it. You say, "Stop it!" but of course he doesn't. So then you say, "Mom, he's breathing too loud." And your mom says, "Stop complaining."

Where is the magnifying glass going to point now? Circle it in the picture at the top of the page.

It is going to point at your mom!

When you have the magnifying glass held tight in your hand, you are going to swing around and point it at anyone or anything that gets in your way. Then that person or that thing is going to seem awful too.

So here's the problem: What if your mom is one of your coaches? If your mom has been reading this book along with you, she probably knows by now that when you are negative, she shouldn't just say, "Stop complaining." Now that she knows about hurdles, she might say, "Jump that hurdle."

Except what are you likely to say? Be honest.

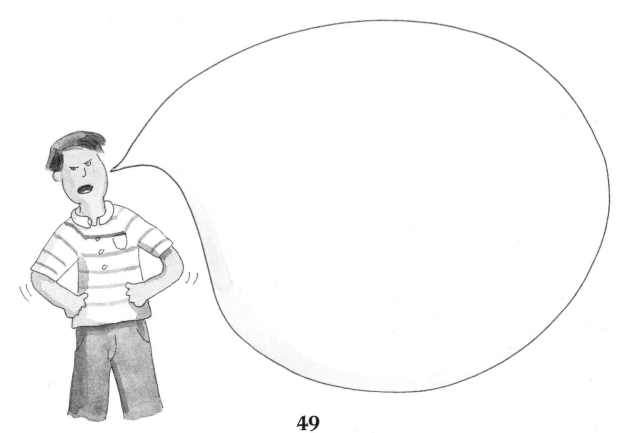

If you are like most kids, you would probably say, "That's stupid." That's because you are annoyed, and you are busy holding the magnifying glass. When the magnifying glass is pointing at your mom, you are likely to think, "She always blames me" or "She doesn't care."

It's going to be hard to listen to your mom, and you're going to feel more like kicking the hurdle than jumping it.

So what should your mom (or other coach) do?

The first thing your coach should do is recognize how you are feeling. In the car example, right after you say, "Mom, he's breathing too loud," the best thing for your mom to say would be something along the lines of, "It sounds like that's really bothering you."

When someone recognizes what you're feeling, you can relax a little. You don't need to grip the magnifying glass as tightly.

Words like

all help you to feel understood. Your coach should use these sorts of words first.

What comes next?

Well, most people don't like to be told what to do. If your coach tells you to "jump the hurdle," you might still feel like arguing, simply because you don't want to be bossed around.

So instead, your coach could try asking a question like, "What do you think you should do?" Or your coach could say, "Remember what you learned about those hurdles?"

For some kids, humor helps, as long as the joke is about those pesky hurdles and not about your trouble handling them.

Some kids like to develop a signal with their coach. You and your coach might agree that your coach is going to wink at you to help you remember about jumping. Or maybe your coach can make a funny face and mouth the word "jump!" Signals are fun, and they give you some privacy while helping you to remember things that are hard to remember when you're busy feeling annoyed.

How can your coach best help you?
What should your coach say or do to remind
you about the things you're learning?

Write your
ideas here.

Exercise #2
Leaving the Past
Behind

Kids who are best at jumping hurdles learn to jump them smoothly. They don't fuss about the hurdle first, and once they have jumped they don't look back.

What would happen if a child jumped a hurdle and then thought, "That was tough. I hated that hurdle. I always have to deal with hurdles. It isn't fair." The child would be so busy grumbling about the hurdle that two bad things would happen.

1: He would continue to feel unhappy, even though he had already gotten past the hurdle.

2: He wouldn't be able to concentrate on the rest of the obstacle course.

But some kids do just that. They get past one of life's hurdles, and then they continue to complain about it.

It's as if these kids are carrying a bad-memories backpack. Every time something bad happens, they stuff it into the backpack and continue to lug it around.

Kids who are negative thinkers tend to carry around this sort of backpack. They can't forget about the bad and unfair things that have happened to them, because all those bad and unfair things are in the bad-memories backpack.

Write down some things that you've been carrying around in your bad-memories backpack. Include the things that bother you even though they happened a long time ago, or even though there is nothing anyone can do about them.

You probably know that bad-memories backpacks are heavy. Carrying them around would make anyone feel negative and grouchy.

What you may not know is that you can decide to put the backpack down.

Imagine yourself taking that heavy backpack off your back and walking away from it. Leave all those bad memories in the backpack, and then leave the backpack behind.

The next time you have a problem, decide how you are going to solve it. (Hint: jump!) Once you've solved it, there is no need to stuff it into the bad-memories backpack. Remember, the backpack isn't even on your back anymore!

Where would be a good place to leave your bad-memories backpack? Draw it.

Keep the bad-memories backpack off your back, and keep your eyes focused ahead. It's a whole lot easier to get through life that way.

It's also a lot more fun.

Exercise #3
Flip Your Brain

If you're practicing jumping hurdles every day, and if you've left your bad-memories backpack on page 59, where it belongs, you probably notice you're beginning to feel better. Your brain is becoming more flexible, and you aren't feeling so stuck.

But sometimes, even when kids are working on jumping hurdles and letting bad memories go, negative thoughts still come crowding into their brain when something goes wrong.

You don't get to decide which thoughts are going to pop into your head. But the good news is: You do get to decide how you're going to respond to those thoughts.

Remember that some brains naturally pull toward the negative. If you have a brain that pulls toward the negative, it's time to teach your brain to steer toward the positive instead. You can do this by learning to "flip" your brain.

Pretend that the circles on this page are the two sides of a coin. "Heads" stands for positive thoughts and "tails" stands for negative thoughts. Decorate the positive and negative sides of the coin.

Now go find a real coin. Flip it. Did it land on heads or on tails?

Flip it again. And again.

Sometimes the coin lands on heads, and sometimes it lands on tails. Your brain is like that, too. Sometimes it will land on the good parts of a situation, and you will feel happy. Sometimes it will land on the bad parts of a situation, and you will feel angry or sad.

But you can learn to flip your brain, just like you flip a coin.

When your mind goes to the bad parts of a situation, you can grumble about it, like you used to. Or you can decide that grumbling is a waste of time and that you are going to do something else instead.

That's right. You have the power to choose.

You can flip your brain by deciding to think about the good parts instead.

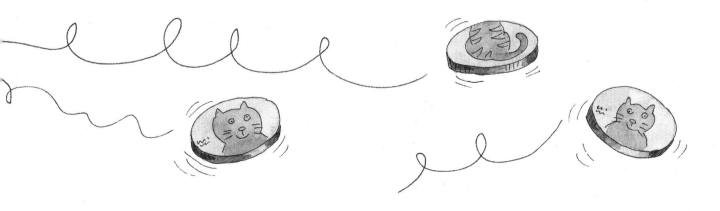

See if you can figure out something good to think about in each of these situations.

Your teacher brought sleds for the class to use at recess, but the principal just announced that it is too cold to go outside.

You love brownies, but your brother ate the last one.

You are right in the middle of a computer game when your dad says it's time for bed.

It's OK to feel sad or mad about a situation that isn't working out the way you want it to. Those feelings are natural.

But if you stay focused on the bad parts, the bad parts don't change to good parts. The only thing that happens is that you stay unhappy. So staying focused on the bad parts doesn't help you at all.

Tell yourself, "I don't like what is happening, but I have to find a way to deal with it." Then flip your brain.

Imagine your brain coin spinning through the air and landing on heads this time. Pick out something good to focus on. Or figure out how you're going to deal with the situation, and focus on that instead.

Over the next few days, see if you can find some opportunities to practice flipping your brain.

Exercise #4
The High-Five Game

What happens when you flip your brain and the heads side comes up blank? Sometimes, especially when you're upset, it's hard to notice anything good.

The high-five game will strengthen the positive side of your brain, teaching it to notice what is good.

To play the game, you are going to think of a situation that really bothers you. Then make a fist. The fist shows how you feel when you're focused on the bad parts of a situation (angry!).

Next, think of one good thing you can focus on instead. When you think of a good thing, you get to lift up one finger.

Now think of another good thing, and raise another finger.

Keep going until you have all five fingers up. Then give a high-five to the grown-up you are with, or use your hand to pat yourself on the back.

I'LL SAVE MY ALLOWANCE AND HAVE $5 SOON

Your coach (your mom or dad or some other grown-up) can help you think of positive things. The only rule is that the positive things have to relate to the situation you feel grumbly about, not just things that make you happy in general.

For example, you're at the ice cream store with your best friend on a hot summer day, and they are all out of your favorite chocolate chip cookie dough flavor.

COUNTS

◎ I've always wanted to try
   chocolate peanut butter cup. Yum!
◎ This ice cream will cool me off.
◎ My best friend just told a funny joke.
◎ The guy at the ice cream counter is nice.
◎ I'll get some sprinkles, too.

DOESN'T COUNT

◎ We're having pizza for dinner.
◎ My neighbor's dog is totally cool.
◎ No school for four more weeks!
◎ Shooting hoops this morning was fun.
◎ Next weekend we're going to the beach.

DOESN'T EVEN COME CLOSE TO COUNTING

I guess I can choke down a different flavor if I have to.

Now you try the game. Read the situation described below.

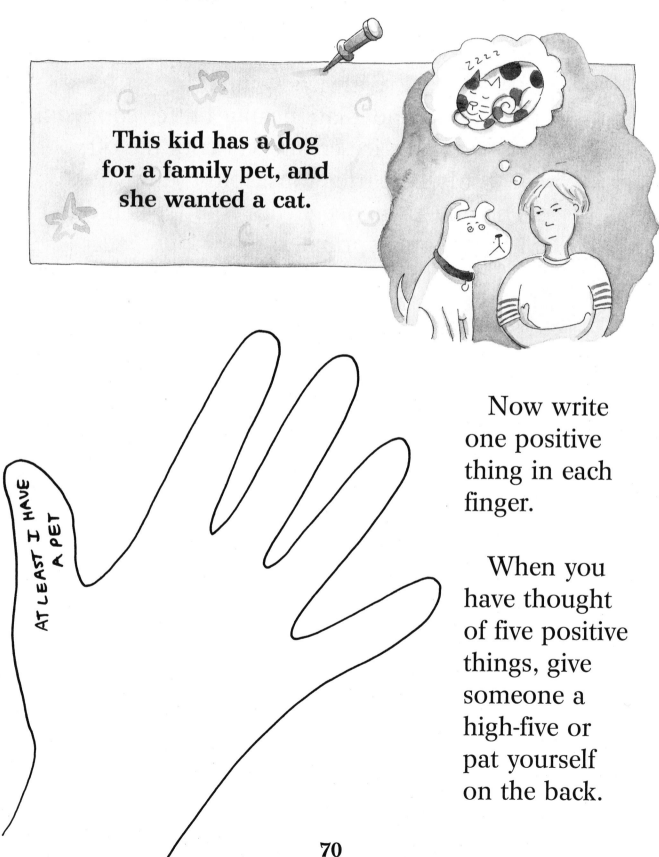

This kid has a dog for a family pet, and she wanted a cat.

AT LEAST I HAVE A PET

Now write one positive thing in each finger.

When you have thought of five positive things, give someone a high-five or pat yourself on the back.

What is something you've been grumbling about? Write your situation here.

Now think of five positive things you could be focusing on.

Whenever you want to flip to the positive side of a situation, but you need help figuring out what the positive side is, you can play the high-five game.

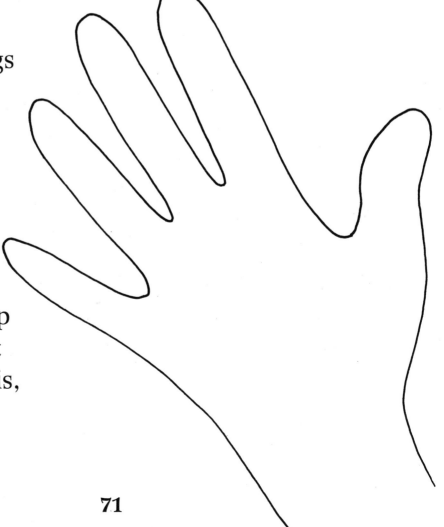

CHAPTER TEN

What If Anger Gets in the Way?

Negative thinking leads to anger. For some kids, this happens right away. They think "no fair!" or "I hate this!" and then **BAM**, they are mad.

How quickly do you get angry? Circle your answer on this scale.

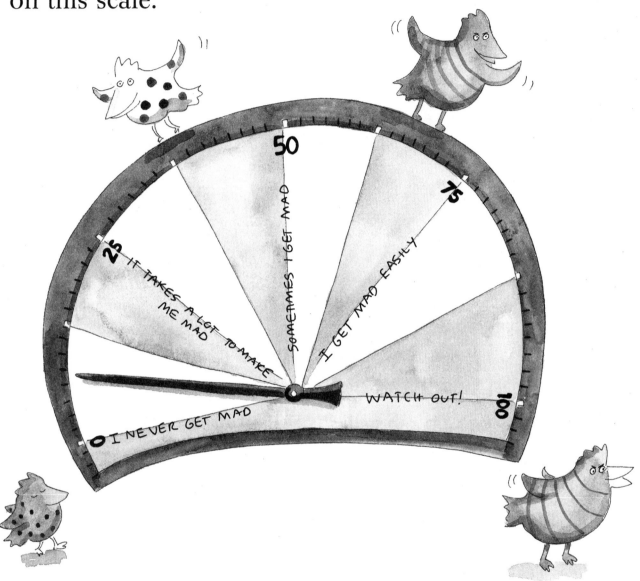

Anger makes the part of your brain that knows how to think clearly shut down.

So if you're a kid who gets angry right away, you are probably going to need to calm down before you can do any of the exercises described in this book.

Taking a break is a great way to calm down. Taking a break means not looking at the positive or the negative. It means stepping away from the whole situation so that your mind and your body can recover.

It might be tempting to continue to grumble while you're taking a break. Try not to do that. Tell yourself, "I'm taking a break, I'll get back to that later." Then try to shift your mind to something else.

Some kids take a break by reading a book.

Others take a break by shooting baskets.

Think about what helps you when you're angry.

Do you need to do something relaxing like drawing pictures or watching TV?

Or do you need to do something active, like playing with your dog or riding your bike?

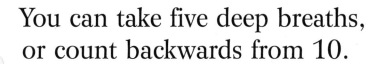

Taking a break is also something you can do in your mind.

You can take five deep breaths, or count backwards from 10.

You can imagine your problems drifting away in a hot air balloon.

Or you can think about one of your favorite things.

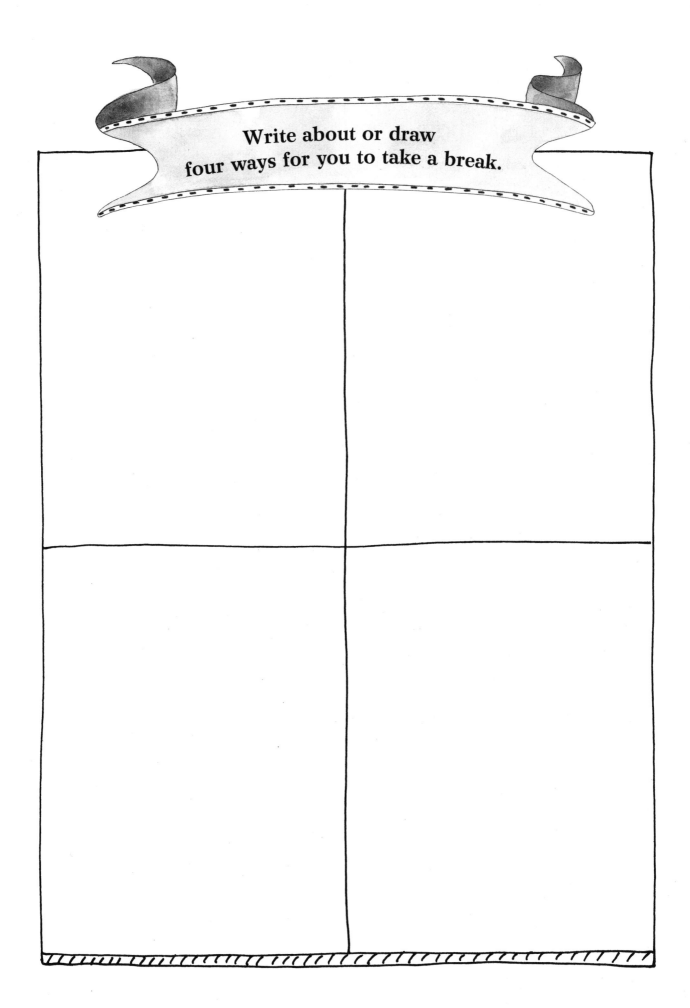

Write about or draw
four ways for you to take a break.

Some people think that taking a break is a bad thing. They say you should "face your problems" and not avoid them.

But if you think about it, when you're stuck in a negative mood, you aren't facing your problems in a useful way. Instead, you are only complaining about them. Complaining can last a long time, and in lots of ways it makes things worse.

Taking a break helps you to calm down. It's like pausing for a deep breath before stepping up to bat.

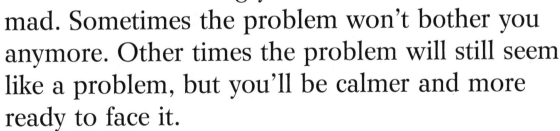

Of course, eventually you'll need to return to whatever was making you mad. Sometimes the problem won't bother you anymore. Other times the problem will still seem like a problem, but you'll be calmer and more ready to face it.

How to
Stay Positive

Now that you've learned how to turn your attention from the negative to the positive, it's important to keep the positive side of your brain strong.

One way to do this is to continue to practice the brain exercises in this book, even after you already know them all.

Another way is to think about the positive things in your life every day.

Do you have a favorite photograph, one that you love looking at because it reminds you of a happy time? Looking at photos and remembering stories from happy times helps us to feel good. It strengthens the positive side of the brain.

You can create a favorite-memories folder in your mind. Your favorite-memories folder will hold memories of times when you felt especially happy or proud.

Write about or draw a memory that you could put into your favorite-memories folder right now.

You can add more memories to the folder in your mind as time goes by.

A third way to stay positive is by noticing the good things that happen every day. Maybe your friend saved a seat for you at lunch. Maybe your dad came home early from work. Maybe your dog listened to a command for the first time ever.

GOOD BOY!

Sometimes people forget to talk about the good things that are happening in their lives. Talking about the good things helps you feel happier, and it makes the people around you happier, too.

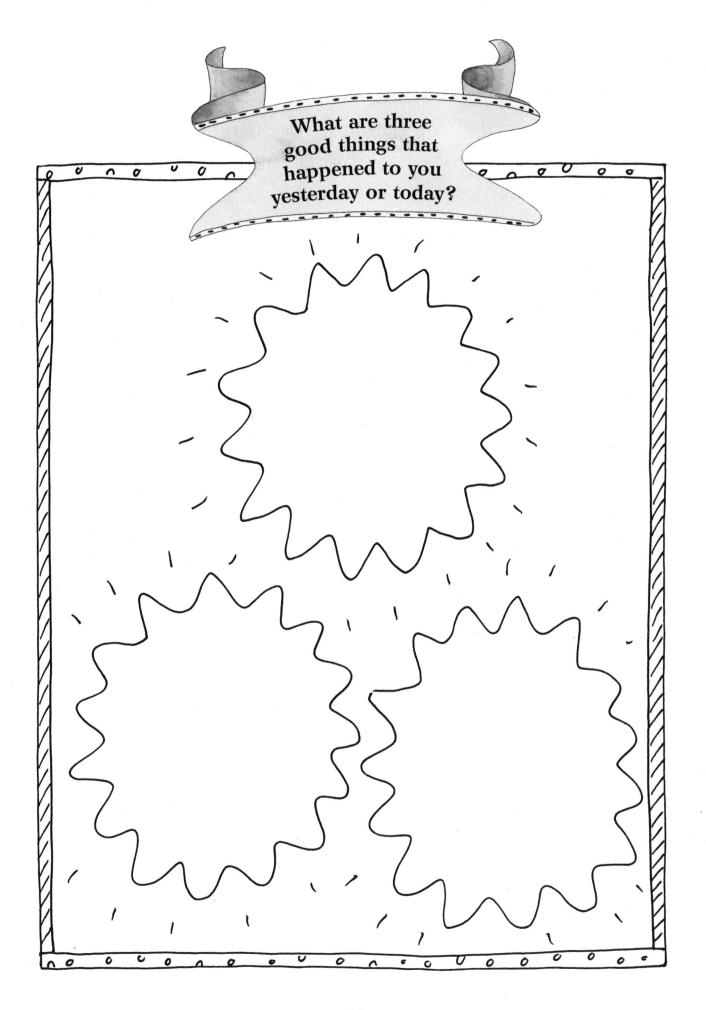

What are three good things that happened to you yesterday or today?

In the car, at dinnertime, at bedtime (anytime you can!), talk to the grown-ups in your life. Tell them what you're interested in, what you've been thinking about, and the funny or good things that happened to you that day.

Your mom and dad (or other coaches) can ask you questions that will help you notice these positive things. Here are some examples of questions that will steer your brain toward the positive:

WHAT IS SOMETHING FUNNY THAT HAPPENED TODAY?

WHAT IS SOMETHING YOU ARE PROUD OF?

WHAT DID YOU DO AT RECESS?

WHAT IS THE BEST PART OF YOUR DAY?

WHAT WOULD YOU LIKE TO LEARN MORE ABOUT?

WHAT IS YOUR FAVORITE GAME?

At first, you might not be able to think of answers to these questions. Some kids aren't used to talking about themselves, or they are used to talking only about problems.

If your mom and dad keep asking these kinds of questions, though, they will help you strengthen the positive parts of your mind. Your answers will help your mom and dad get to know you better, too.

You can still talk about problems when you need help solving them. That's important. You just don't want to spend too much time grumbling.

Spend a little bit of time talking about problems and lots of time talking about the things that are interesting and fun in your life.

You Can Do It!

Do you remember when you first learned how to do subtraction, or how to write your name in cursive? It was probably hard. Learning a new skill takes lots of practice. Learning to shift away from negative thoughts will take practice, too.

Right now, negative thoughts pop into your brain quickly and easily. Positive thoughts might be hard to find. But if you practice the brain exercises over and over again, really concentrating on what is going on inside your head, you will begin to notice something: The brain exercises get easier.

When something goes wrong, it won't be such a big deal. Problems that used to take up lots of time (because you would argue and complain, and then get yelled at and sometimes end up in trouble) will get solved pretty quickly.

You won't be holding on to that weird magnifying glass, so the bad things won't seem unusually large. It will be easier to focus on the good parts. And in time, you will begin to feel better.

SO REMEMBER...

🌀 Jump those hurdles.

🌀 Leave the bad-memories backpack behind.

🌀 Flip your brain.

🌀 Play the high-five game.

🌀 Open your favorite-memories folder.

🌀 Stay focused on the positive.

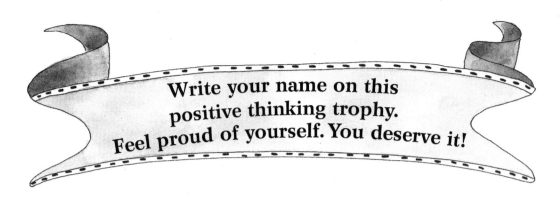

Write your name on this
positive thinking trophy.
Feel proud of yourself. You deserve it!

It's going to feel so good!